CONSECRATION OF THE ALEPH BET

by Leonor Scliar-Cabral
translated by Alexis Levitin

Ben Yehuda Press
Teaneck, New Jersey

CONSECRATION OF THE ALEPH BET © 2025 Alexis Levitin. Original Portuguese *Sagração do Alfabeto* © 2009 Leonor Scliar-Cabral. All rights reserved. No part of this book may be used or reproduced in any manner whatsoever without written permission except in the case of brief quotations embodied in critical articles and reviews.

Published by Ben Yehuda Press
122 Ayers Court #1B
Teaneck, NJ 07666

http://www.BenYehudaPress.com

To subscribe to our monthly book club and support independent Jewish publishing, visit https://www.patreon.com/BenYehudaPress

Jewish Poetry Project #50   **http://jpoetry.us**

Ben Yehuda Press books may be purchased at a discount by synagogues, book clubs, and other institutions buying in bulk. For information, please email markets@BenYehudaPress.com

Cover illustration by Nick Levitin

ISBN13 978-1-963475-54-8

Library of Congress Cataloging-in-Publication Data

Names: Scliar-Cabral, Leonor, 1929- author | Levitin, Alexis translator | Scliar-Cabral, Leonor, 1929- SagracÌ§aÌƒo do alfabeto. | Scliar-Cabral, Leonor, 1929- SagracÌ§aÌƒo do alfabeto. English
Title: Consecration of the aleph bet / by Leonor Scliar-Cabral ; translated by Alexis Levitin.
Description: Teaneck, New Jersey : Ben Yehuda Press, 2025. | Series: Jewish poetry project ; #50 | "Original Portuguese SagracÌ§aÌƒo do Alfabeto Â© 2009 Leonor Scliar-Cabral"--Title page verso. | Summary:"Consecration of the Aleph Bet is a bilingual Portuguese/English collection of 22 sonnets, one each for each letter of the Hebrew alphabet. The poems engage with Jewish history and spirituality"-- Provided by publisher.
Identifiers: LCCN 2025006577 | ISBN 9781963475548 paperback
Subjects: LCSH: Scliar-Cabral, Leonor, 1929---Translations into English | Hebrew language--Alphabet--Poetry | LCGFT: Sonnets
Classification: LCC PQ9698.29.C544 S2413 2025 | DDC 869.1/42--dc23/eng/20250429
LC record available at https://lccn.loc.gov/2025006577

*Dedico esse livro aos artesãos anônimos que,
no Monte Sinai, efetuaram a façanha de unir um hieróglifo
ao som inicial de uma palavra, na escrita acronímica,
primeiro passo para a futura escrita alfabética.*

*I dedicate this book to the anonymous craftsmen who,
on Mount Sinai, performed the feat of joining a hieroglyph
to the initial sound of a word, in acronymic writing,
the first step towards a future of alphabetic writing.*

Contents

Acknowledgments	ix
The Kabbalistic (and Brilliant) Poetry of Leonor Scliar-Cabral	x
א ALEF / ALEPH	2
ב BET / BET	6
ג GUÍMEL / GIMEL	10
ד DALET / DALET	14
ה HÊ / HEI	18
ו VAV / VAV	22
ז ZÁYIN / ZAYIN	26
ח HET / HET	30
ט TET / TET	34
י YOD / YUD	38
כ KAF / KAF	42
ל LAMED / LAMED	46
מ MEM / MEM	50
נ NUN / NUN	54
ס SAMEKH / SAMECH	58
ע ÁYIN / AYIN	62
פ PÊ / PEI	66
צ TSADÊ / TZADI	70
ק QOF / KUF	74
ר RESH / RESH	78
ש SHIN / SHIN	82
ת TAV / TAV	86
Implicit Voices in *Consecration of the Aleph Bet*	89
Bibliographic Reference	93
Translating *Consecration of the Aleph Bet*: The Joys of Exigency	94
About the Author and Translator	97

Acknowledgments

I would like to give warm thanks to the esteemed Brazilian poet and linguist Leonor Scliar-Cabral, who gave me shelter years ago, while we worked together on these translations. Her diligence, patience, sense-of-humor, and imagination contributed enormously to the final shaping of these twenty-two rhymed sonnets in English. We both felt that adherence to the rigorous demands of the sonnet form would be essential to any successful translation. As a result, all liberties taken to arrive at natural, harmonious sonnets in English were carefully considered by the poet and were given her approval. It was a delight working with her.

I would also like to thank the editors of the following magazines, who published individual poems from this collection:
Amethyst Review
Blue Unicorn
Epoch
Home Planet News
Measure
 niv
Oberon Poetry Magazine
Per Contra
Plume
Poetica Magazine

The Kabbalistic (and Brilliant) Poetry of Leonor Scliar-Cabral

Cousin, friend, admirer (and even disciple) of Leonor Scliar-Cabral, I have accompanied her career since childhood. We come from a family of cultured and talented people (Esther, Leonor's sister, was a great pianist and composer; Carlos, our cousin, was a great plastic artist, as was Salomon, who was a noted photographer) and among all that talent, Leonor held a prominent position, due especially to her knowledge of and research in the areas of literature and linguistics. It was, however, with a certain surprise when, years ago, I received from Leonor her first poems. Surprise and worry. Usually poets begin early, Castro Alves being the best example of this in Brazil. The idea has developed that poetry is fed by the vigor of youth (or of adolescence), as opposed to fiction, which is the product of maturity: "No one becomes a novelist before the age of forty" is an aphorism I have often heard. Leonor was young, naturally (she never stops being young: she clearly has discovered the Fountain of Youth) but she began her poetic trajectory at an unusual age, and that awakened my fears: wasn't that attempt a mistake on her part?

With great joy I discovered that, in fact, it was not a mistake. On the contrary, it was an extraordinary revelation, an explosion of talent. I am not a poetry critic; my response to a poetic text is merely instinctive, visceral. But at that moment I felt absolutely certain that I was facing a great poet.

And now, that same certainty is repeating itself, years later, as I face *the Consecration of the Aleph Bet* which, I do not hesitate to say, is one of the most beautiful and original poetic projects that I have known. Coming together here are not only Leonor's poetic vocation, but also her broad linguistic culture, as well as Jewish tradition—which, in her case, does not spring from a religious, but rather an historical and cultural source. In a certain way, Leonor is recovering the tradition of the Kabbala, which, as we know, gave value to each and every letter, seeing in them hidden powers.

But the Kabbalists did this through numerology; Leonor, does not. She rediscovers in each letter its symbolic history and uses that as an inspiration for her poems. Which, as the first of them says, "Aleph," naturally, (which Borges, author of a book by that very title, would have given a standing ovation), "rise up… to burst apart the mysteries of time." Just as she writes how "scribes revive prophetic words divine, on pure papyrus," she herself revives poetic traditions both ancient and profound. And she does so, we should note, in a completely appropriate way, using the sonnet, which many young poets today consider obsolete. But it is not, just as the letters themselves are not, (rarely have they been so glorified), nor the text itself.

Consecration of the Aleph Bet is a consecration of Leonor Scliar-Cabral. A consecration that is a great joy for all of us, her readers and her fans, and a joy for the letters themselves: look carefully at those that are typed out here and you will notice that they, too, are giving her a standing ovation.

Moacyr Scliar

ALEF

Com ímpeto os chifres rompem ígneos
os enigmas do tempo enquanto o escriba
sobre o papiro virgem reaviva
do fundo da memória os vaticínios:

Carregarás na areia teus desígnios
para que a voz divina sobreviva
além do mar rompido à deriva,
cravando a ferro e fogo teus domínios.

Ao som inaugural de uma palavra
imprimirás a letra como um selo.
A parte evoca o todo e o elo lavra

as frases e a história com que narras
como D'us te exortou em seu apelo
de fixares eternas as amarras.

ALEPH

Horns rise up with force, igneous, aglow,
to burst apart the mysteries of time,
while scribes revive prophetic words, divine,
on pure papyrus, salvaged long ago.

You'll carry through the sands your great design
so that the holy voice will always be
alive, beyond the wild sundered sea,
as you your realm with sword and flame define.

Each word's initial sound will henceforth be
inscribed by you, a letter like a seal.
The part calls forth the whole and so the script

becomes a tale, as sentences depict
how G-d called out, encouraging your zeal
to fix your ties for all eternity.

ב

BET

Pelos portais da casa tens acesso
à lareira que espalha noite e dia
o calor protetor da mãe judia
pelas quatro paredes do recesso.

Braços em rotação, lento processo
das retas na procura de outras vias
até se recurvarem, seios guias,
abrigo de outros símbolos impressos,

cunhados por escribas em tijolos,
em rolos, em papiros, pergaminhos.
Abóbada celeste, em seu colo,

em íntimo convívio, às consoantes,
eternizando as falas em aninho,
reúnem-se as vozes dominantes.

BET

Now through the entrance of the house you come
unto the fire always pulsing heat
and giving forth maternal Jewish warmth
to all four sheltering walls of that retreat.

The turning of the arms, the slow advance
in search of other ways for those straight lines,
until they come curved back, with breasts as guides,
the refuge now of other written signs

first printed out by scribes who wrote on clay
and then on scrolls, papyrus and on parchment.
Celestial vault, close nestled on your breast,

with intimate companionship's caress,
immortalizing sheltered utterance,
vowels join at last their consonants to stay.

GUÍMEL

Ultrapassas as portas, as fronteiras
no lombo do camelo. Inconformada
ou perseguida, irrompes transformada,
cruzando o *Mare Nostrum*, companheira

de outras letras, fiel, a hospedeira.
Previdente, na bolsa armazenada,
a reserva vital purificada
borrifa para sempre as videiras.

Semicírculo, lua decrescente,
valores tripartidos submetidos
ao gesto das vogais proeminente,

ora para trás, ora para frente,
alterando o traçado convertido,
ressuscitando ângulos tangentes.

GIMEL

You go through doorways and you cross frontiers
astride a camel's back. Dissatisfied,
harassed, you burst forth in a new-made guise,
and cross the *Mare Nostrum* without fears,

friend, host to letters of another kind.
Prudent, with rounded pouch well fortified,
your vital reservoir now purified,
you sprinkle for all time the spreading vines.

Waning moon, semicircle of a cowl,
a scattering of values forced to bow
to gestures of predominating vowels,

at times ahead and then at times behind,
an altering, converting shape and sign,
resuscitating straight tangential lines.

DALET

É o delta que se abre majestoso,
portal acolhedor do falo ereto,
triângulo ou quadrado irrequieto
com a chave do mistério pressagioso.

Seio hospedeiro, és seio amoroso
que acalenta o egresso sob seu teto
e o reconduz ao ninho mais secreto,
cálice do ungüento capitoso.

O enlace adoça em mel a aresta dura,
transformada em côncava na Etrúria,
para abraçar a reta em ferradura.

Mas o delta ressurge transportado
do Sinai ao Egeu na voz augúria
de Safo e de Alceu eternizados.

DALET

To welcome in with majesty the straight
phallus to its restless triangle or square,
that key to mystery, that promised lair,
the delta opens wide its inner gate.

Hospitable breast, you, the loving breast
that warms the son returned to native soil,
and leads him back to the most secret nest,
that chalice of intoxicating oil.

Sweet clasp of honey sweetens the sharp stroke,
transformed in Etruria to curve concave,
in horseshoe nest the straight line is embraced.

But then the delta reappears, evoked
from Sinai to Egypt, in prophetic staves
immortalized by Sappho and Alcaeus.

HÊ

Em oração, os braços levantados
para o céu, na cadência o sopro espiram.
Cravaram a navalha e suprimiram
a cabeça e o corpo ajoelhado.

Os olhos baixam do Inominado
e à direita e à esquerda o outro miram,
buscando a identidade a que aspiram:
em profano o orar é transformado.

O vertical agora é horizontal,
três traços paralelos numa haste
que selam o registro umbilical

da voz em solo grego: consoantes
e vogais costuradas em contraste
nas cirandas infindas das bacantes.

HEI

With arms uplifted towards the sky they pray,
exhaling rhythmic cadence with their breath.
Then drawing razor deep they cut away
both head and body, leaving arms bereft.

From the Ineffable their eyes now turn
and left and right all gaze upon their peers,
to find the final self they hope to earn:
and prayer settles in the human sphere.

The vertical turned horizontal now,
three strokes in parallel upon a line
that seal the borrowed record and allow

the voice to speak on Grecian soil: bacchants
who sow their vowels and consonants in time,
contrasted in their endless circle dance.

ו

VAV

Esôfago, traquéia, remo ou falo,
vais singrando a corrente ao estuário
dos rios que se encontram no fadário
de fugirem das margens em gargalo,

submissos ao destino sem quebrá-lo,
morrendo e renascendo, refratários
a não sobreviver. Duro calvário
do fígado exposto e ser vassalo

das bicadas eternas. Nas papilas,
nos olhos, nos ouvidos e narinas,
na derme, nas entranhas tu asilas

a energia cósmica: no jogo
dos gestos em espelho, a divina
letra no tetragrama a ferro e fogo.

VAV

Esophagus, trachea, phallus, oar,
you join the rivers rushing toward the sea
and ride their currents toward your destiny
through narrow funneled straits and rocky shores

submissive to their unrelenting fate
of dying and of being born again,
of clasping life. A Calvary of pain,
that of the naked liver's harsh mandate:

eternal thrusting beaks. Now, to your tongue,
your ears and eyes, your nostrils flaring wide,
and to your skin and to your entrails come

cosmic energies: in the mirrored game
of gestures, sacred and now sanctified
piece of tetragrammaton, forged in flame.

ZÁYIN

Defrontam-se os guerreiros na batalha
entre a tese e a antítese, entre o bem
contra o mal, entre o apoio e o desdém,
paralelas opostas por navalhas

que desferem os golpes e retalham
as hostes inimigas e detêm-se
diante da diagonal enfim refém
das pontas sobrepostas que a entalham.

Durante sete luas pelo obscuro
mar, a quilha fenícia o reversível
traçado vacilante e inseguro

vai semeando com os dedos espalmados:
só o que a pupila vê, o inacessível
e sua infinita tela descartados.

ZAYIN

With thesis and antithesis at war,
with good and evil grappling hand to hand,
between the battle lines these warriors stand,
opposing forces raising sharpened swords

that flash and slash, that parry and that smite
a host of enemies, but then must halt
before that slanting line their blind assault.
A zigzag trap imprisons both the knights.

A long Phoenician keel with fanning oars
for seven moons plows through the darkened seas
and spreads with open palms on alien shores

an indecisive but recorded line.
It only tells of what their eyes can see.
It may not touch upon what is divine.

HET

Barreira, muro ou grade, dominó,
tu abafas a voz subentendida
da qual depende a concha escolhida
para ouvir. Amordaça-nos o agora,

prisioneiros que somos como Jó
dos espaços estreitos, da guarida
sem futuro, da ação sempre impedida
pelos braços atados. O algoz

é o relógio imutável do mutismo,
condenando-a à prisão de ser silente
ou de ser a vassala do grafismo

da letra precedente. Garroteados,
só o porvir liberta essa torrente
subterrânea e o fogo represados.

HET

A barrier of iron bars, a wall,
a domino, a cage whose sides surround
and block our voice and smother sound.
The present stifles any cry or call.

Like Job, we're prisoners of straightened spaces.
Our actions always thwarted, arms bound tight,
we struggle to be heard, to claim our right,
but see no hope before our voiceless faces.

Our hangman is a silent clock, stopped dead,
condemning us to silence in our cell
or servitude to letters that precede

and govern us. Garroted, we gaze ahead:
what is to come, alone, may break the spell:
our hidden torrent with its fire freed.

ט

TET

A pele das serpentes acoberta
os escudos e a cruz então entalha
na aliança circular. Frágil muralha,
a letra do Decálogo deserta,

esquecida, e retorna descoberta
em Biblos, no Egeu, de onde se espalha
até o Mar do Norte ou se agasalha
na Terra Santa, curvas entreabertas

como galhos erguidos que retraçam
o cativeiro de sóbolos rios.
Imperceptível sopro que perpassa

entre dentes e língua, intersticial,
como entre folhas tímido cicio:
apaga-se o traço vertical."

TET

They stretch the skins of snakes upon their shields
and then they set a cross imbedded in
the tight-drawn ring. A bulwark, fragile, thin,
a letter that the Decalogue concealed,

ignored, but now returning to be found
in Byblos and in Greece, from where it spread
to Northern Seas or hid itself instead
back in the Holy Land, a curve unbound,

like upraised, arching branches that still grieve
that riverine enmeshed captivity.
A breath that passes almost unperceived,

and, furtive, slips between the teeth and tongue,
rustling leaves, whispers of timidity.
Vertical gone, the cross is now undone.

YOD

Em oferenda a mão, o antebraço,
dorso da língua contra cartilagem,
ou papiro abrindo a ramagem
para perder as folhas passo a passo.

Braço violento erguido no espaço,
ou pacificadora tatuagem
da mão voltada ao chão, hirta barragem
à travessia, ou alças em abraço,

ou mãos em desespero, implorando
clemência, o mesmo signo travestido
dos arabescos vai se despojando.

Um simples traço basta. É a reta
em espelho dos lábios distendidos
que sobre a dura pedra se projeta.

YUD

Extended arm, a hand like a reprieve,
mouth's roof, a tongue against its cartilage.
Papyrus spreading wide its foliage,
then, one by one, the loss of all its leaves.

An arm of violence raised up in space,
or else a soothing image of a hand
pressed to the earth, a rigid ban
to passage, or an arabesque's embrace.

Or hands in desperation, offering pleas
for clemency, the same sign being stripped
of frills and all its former fripperies.

A simple stroke. That's all. A line alone
that serves as mirror to extended lips,
a slash that cuts across unbending stone.

כ

KAF

O dorso reclinado sobre a areia
imprime com as palmas seu traçado
desde o princípio ao fim predestinado.
Matriz multiplicada em tênues veias,

libélulas tremulam e semeiam
o pólen das canções, o som dos bardos
para impedir que morram deslembrados
e para sempre tecem sua teia.

Milagre contra o tempo, contra o alado
murmúrio ou bramido, versos ditos
que o vento leva ao túmulo calado

onde jazem no limbo do segredo.
Milagre que registra no granito
restos da mão impressa, apenas dedos.

KAF

Although a body stretched once on the sand,
the impress of its palm alone remained,
predestined sign upon predestined land,
a matrix for disseminating change,

as dragonflies ashimmer start to spread
the pollen of new songs, for bards to blend,
so they will not be lost among the dead,
and so the weave of words will never end.

A miracle atemporal in history,
unlike all murmured, merely spoken, rhymes
the wind bears off to tombs where silence reigns,

where they lie down in limbo's mystery:
this sign carved now in granite for all times.
From ancient palm prints, these abstract remains.

LAMED

Sou um velho senhor, mas nada vi.
Dependuro-me à corda e me projeto
no espaço, aguilhoado e inquieto
em resgatar os sonhos que traí.

Rebusco na esfinge o que encobri
nos imprecisos traços, arquiteto
de quimeras, o mal formado feto
que na insônia eu mesmo concebi.

E, náufrago perdido em noite escura,
uma réstia emerge, uma esperança:
uma inscrição em gancho me segura,

recolhe-me do abismo em que navego
e me retorna ao solo. Na balança,
o fiel do equilíbrio, calmo e cego.

LAMED

Although I'm old, I haven't seen a thing.
I hang there on my rope. I'm not afraid.
Provoked and anxious, into space I fling
myself, to ransom dreams I once betrayed.

I seek upon the sphinx what I once hid
with tangled, muddled, twisted strokes when I,
as architect of chimeras, undid,
insomniac, good seeds with clever lies.

A castaway, lost in the darkest night,
I glimpse a scrap of hope, a tiny gleam,
a line, a curve, a hook to set things right,

to save me from the depths in which I sail
and bring me back to solid earth. The beam
of balance, calm, blind, steady on the scale.

מ

MEM

Nos degraus da mikvá, pé ante pé,
a letra em ziguezague, ondulação,
movimento contínuo, ablução
dos pecados expulsos pela fé.

Pureza no mergulho inteiro até
a cabeça que escuta a pregação
dos eleitos em santa procissão:
Moisés, o Messias, Maomé.

Balbucio inicial, ritmo infante
sugando o leite morno da nascente
em gestos repetidos, anelantes:

a invocação da mãe. De onde vim?
Para que mar me levam? A torrente
jamais corre igual até os confins.

MEM

She drifts down to the *mikva*, step by step,
a zigzag letter with its waving curves,
its gentle lapping motion, water's purge
of every sin, if faith be truly kept.

Immersed in utter purity, her head
submerged, still echoing with sacred matter
spoken by a line of holy masters:
Moses, Messiah, Mohammad.

First babblings, a child's rhythmic sound
while suckling from its warm initial spring
in longing repetitions of profound

desire, calling: "Mother, where am I from?
And where am I going? And what will it bring?
This rushing river's flow, this endless foam?"

ב

NUN

Enguia que desliza sinuosa
roçando levemente nos corais:
sobem borbulhas, rastros de sinais,
emersos das areias misteriosas,

leito nupcial, alcova veludosa
onde peixes, anêmonas, cristais
polvilham com reflexos siderais
as pétalas e escamas luminosas.

Cordão umbilical, germe da vida,
metade da centena, guardião
que nos protege, dá-nos a guarida

contra pragas e pestes, contra o mau
olhado e, pendente ao coração,
nos reconduz ao âmago vital.

NUN

The eel slips by with sinuosity
and gently skims across the coral's spine:
bubbles of air drift up, a trail of signs
rising from sands of muted mystery,

a nuptial bed, a velvet alcove where
the petals of anemones, the scales
of fish, dusted with phosphorescent veils,
reflect a starlight not from anywhere.

The seed of life, the snake-like cord, the cry,
cabala's half a hundred, standing guard,
a shield protecting us from the unknown,

from plagues and pestilence, the evil eye,
and, firmly lodged, a pledge above our heart,
conducting us in safety to our home.

ס

SAMEKH

Treliça de arbustos, cedro ou linho,
ou peixe sem a cauda, decepado,
esqueleto invisível, o calado
apoio que sustenta nos caminhos

os passos mensageiros, adivinhos
da Terra Prometida, o quadrado
em círculo perfeito transmudado,
ou a cruz, como pás de um moinho

movidas pelo vento, xis fixado,
expressando a imprevista mutação
ao jogador perplexo, desnorteado,

de um xadrez sem juízes nem sintaxe.
Embaixatriz de sons sem conexão,
rodopiando num eixo multiface.

SAMECH

A trellis weave, a sheaf of stems and stalks,
or else a fish, with neither head nor tail,
an unseen skeleton that never talks,
but gives support, sustaining on the trail

Those prophets searching for the Promised Land,
diviners seeking the divine. The square
evolves and is replaced. A Hebrew hand
now draws instead a perfect ring. Elsewhere,

the cross embedded in the square breaks free,
revolving in the wind like windmill blades
and turns into an x that now is fixed.

Chess players at their game stare hard, transfixed,
this game is not the one that once they played.
Xerox and xylophone both sound like z.

ע

ÁYIN

Involuntária a órbita oscila
sob invisível pálpebra apagada
e devolve visíveis, deflagradas
as dores ou risadas que titilam

sem disfarce possível. Na pupila
ardente pelas chamas atiçada
irrompem as paixões paramentadas
com manto de safiras que cintilam.

Código de segredos, vais jogando
em volutas anéis, a projeção
da boca oracular, antecipando

o círculo completo, a mandala,
testemunha ocular, a perfeição,
o múltiplo dos múltiplos, cabala.

AYIN

The orbit oscillates without a will
beneath a lashless, extirpated lid,
and makes both pain and laughter visible,
its gaze revealing what it once had hid.

Beyond disguise, the passions now burst free,
the pupil flares, dark coals are stoked to flame,
the eye is decked in dazzling revelry,
the flash of sapphires in an oval frame.

A code of secrets, you roll out your rings
in endless spirals, projecting with your gaze
the oracle, the sacred mouth that sings,

those rounded lips, that circle full, mandala,
the eye now witness, joining all the ways,
the multiple of multiples, kabbalah

פ

PÊ

Pórtico da palavra, inaudível
silêncio que não vive sem a voz,
borbulhas a dançar no ar, após
explodir a cortiça irreversível,

jogada no espaço. Irredutível
a reta se instala e acolhe só
a meia-lua e as duas bordam nós
de letras sobre a linha invisível.

Ângulo do retângulo em arco,
ou novamente ângulo, metáforas
ou pedaços de boca, desembarco

no papiro, papel ou pergaminho
que transportam os signos em diáspora
plantados nos confins e descaminhos.

PEI

Portico of the word, inaudible
silence that cannot live without a voice,
and bubbles dancing in the air, just when
the cork, beyond recall, without a choice,

explodes and flies off into space. Mere stroke,
it takes its place, accepting for its sign
the half-moon as a mate, and both embroider
knots of letters on the unseen line.

Rectangle's angle now begins to curve
or turn again to angle, metaphors
or pieces of a mouth, that come to land

on parchment or papyrus that now serve
to carry off the signs in Diaspora,
and plant them far away on alien sand.

צ

TSADÊ

Arpão, anzol ou âncora vertida,
cravando tuas garras ferrugentas,
à prova das marés e das tormentas.
Acabas prisioneira da ferida

na cratera arenosa invadida
que te envolve sob colcha lamacenta,
máscara indecifrável da ossamenta
dos naufrágios. Rebelde, és investida

de poderes sagrados, e inventas
no enlace com o som novas veredas.
Obstáculo rompido, a marulhenta

passagem nos alvéolos pelas frestas
agora descerradas, alamedas
que se abrem. No final, apenas retas.

TZADI

Harpoon or hook, an anchor overboard,
you fix your rusty claws deep in the sand
and leave the violated bottom scored,
while firm against both tide and storm you stand.

But you are captive to the wound you've made,
as slimy sea-bed blankets wrap you round,
an indecipherable mask for half-decayed
ribs, bones, keels, carcasses of ships long drowned.

A rebel, sacred power now invests
you, opens pathways for your new-made bits
of plosive sound. The dam once burst, it lets

a secret sea sound out, a hiss that fits
through tiny apertures, and now suggests
a tree-lined path. An image sound begets.

QOF

Descemos pelos troncos esfomeados
e surpresos erguemos o olhar
para o horizonte ao longe, céu e mar.
Ecoam vozes, sons desabafados

ao ritmo da artéria, compassados
pelos bastões, estacas a pulsar
contra o solo, marcando nosso andar.
Milhões de anos passam amarrados

à palavra, reféns de passageiras
narrativas, apenas enunciadas,
brasa e cinzas, ao pé de uma fogueira.

Ômega sem alfa, elos já rompidos,
humílima origem renegada,
de nosso irmão sem fala esquecidos.

KUF

Descending famished, we climb down our trees
and in surprise together lift our eyes
to far horizons, distant seas and skies.
Then voices echo, sound at last bursts free

to move in time to the arterial beat,
with staves, with clubs and cudgels, as they pound
our forward progress slowly on the ground.
Years pass in millions, speech their single feat,

but always tied to tales of ancient others,
told mouth to mouth, around the fire's blaze,
from embers pulsing red to silent ash.

Omega without Alpha, linkage slashed,
we turn from humble origins and raze
our dim and half-forgotten speechless brothers.

RESH

Cabeça e recomeço da raiz,
até o fim dos dias o suporte.
Esforço que esmaece seu recorte
e apenas fixa a linha do nariz,

desmemoriada e tênue cicatriz,
unindo o rico e o pobre, a dura morte
e a vida, o fogo e a água, o sul e o norte,
a variação dos sons e seus matizes.

Imperceptível, breve, frágil ponte,
batida leve de asa no arvoredo
ou múltiplo gorjeio de uma fonte,

ou o sussurro surdo, o friccionar
de folhas maceradas pelos dedos,
marulho na garganta a farfalhar.

RESH

This is the head. It says begin again.
It is our mainstay to the end of time.
Its very labor dims its very lines,
it fixes only on the nose and then

turns all into a lost, abstracted scar,
uniting deepest poverty with wealth,
uniting painful death with vibrant health,
uniting tones and hues, the near, the far.

A gentle flutter in a grove of wings,
a something imperceptible and brief,
or else the rippling gurgle of a spring,

or voiceless whispering, an endless note,
like fingers rubbing into dust a leaf:
the wash of waves, a rustle in the throat.

ש

SHIN

Dispara a flecha em sigma e tomba em arco
e modifica o ziguezague dente
em sinuosa onda de serpente.
Os silvos todos une o traço parco

e sobre o pergaminho grava o marco,
resumo dos zumbidos estridentes
ou dos surdos sussurros sós, silentes.
Separadora de águas turvas, barco

a triturar os grãos com afiados
incisivos em ponta. Flamejantes
chamas de candelabro: espalhados

pelas tábuas, respingos descarnados,
gotas de cera, lágrimas serpeantes
de velhos e crianças trucidados.

SHIN

The arrow's sigma flight drops to the ground,
transforming with its arc the zigzag tooth
into a serpent, sinuous and smooth.
Its meager line suggests all hissing sounds,

inscribed on parchment as a shifting sign,
a symbol for all strident sibilations,
or simply silent, subtle susurrations.
A prow that plows the turbid waterline

and grinds grain down with sharp incisor teeth.
A candelabra's flickering, licking flames,
a shape of life and death, of bodies flung

on aged floorboards, splattering a wreath
of dribbled wax, hot tears, the blood-rust stains
of slaughtered elders and the slaughtered young.

TAV

Arco-íris que liga céu e inferno,
percurso que eu percorro e me fraciona
já sem forças: o alento me abandona.
As gotas que eu verti sob o paterno

olhar em Santa Aliança, no eterno
pacto com D'us, no olvido desmoronam.
Eu indago: Por que me decepcionas?
Por que carrego a cruz no negro averno

de buscar meu espaço, conspurcando
cada palmo com sangue de inocentes?
A estrela de Davi está chorando

e a arca tão sagrada se esconde
cada vez mais, alheia, inclemente:
a voz dos patriarcas não responde.

TAV

Rainbow link of holy spheres, lower depths,
this route I follow as it breaks me down,
drained dry, deserted by my inner breath.
The drops I spilled beneath a father's frown

in Holy Covenant, a pact with G-d
eternal, collapsed now to the ground.
I challenge him: Why have you ground me down?
Why must I bear this cross, this long-sought plot

of land, my space in hell, for which I fight
foot by foot, befouled with blood of innocents?
The star of David sheds a silent tear,

the sacred arc now hides its face from sight,
grown alien, distant in its reticence:
the voices of our fathers are not here.

Implicit Voices in *Consecration of the Aleph Bet*

In *Consecration of the Aleph Bet*, I wish to pay tribute to one of mankind's major accomplishments in its struggle for knowledge: the invention of the alphabet. The development of the written recording of experience follows a slow trajectory from the predominantly pictographic phase (involving the mimetic translation of the reality of the world), through the ideogram, characterized by metaphor and metonymy, till it reaches phonographic writing, which represents speech. Phonographic writing can be syllabic or approximately phonemic, in which case one or more letters represent a class of sounds, that is to say, phonemes. It must be made clear that some hieroglyphic systems incorporated phonographic signs for the purpose of distinguishing differing meanings for the same representation. To complicate matters, a single system of writing could make use of different fonts or scripts, as in the case of the Greek, Cyrillic, Latin, Gothic, Hebrew and Arabic alphabets. Those alphabets, then, could be applied to different languages. What determines the value of letters in a given alphabet in a specific language are its orthographic conventions.

In truth, the precursors of writing can be found in Mesopotamia and in Egypt. In the case of the former, they can be found on small stones or clay tablets, generally serving as records for accounts and coinciding with Sumerian pictograms. While cuneiform writing was used in the beginning to record names and quantities required for commercial transactions, in Egypt it appears in temple inscriptions of a sacred character. The phonographic signs in the Egyptian system, which will be used again by the Jews on Mount Sinai, are consonantal.

I have tried in this series of twenty-two sonnets to give homage to the lost link between the hieroglyphs and the Phoenician alphabet, that is to say, the proto-Sinaic script, whose earliest manifestation around 1400A.C. appears on a small sandstone sphinx dedicated to the goddess Hathor (recent research reveals the existence of older examples of a similar script, discovered in central Egypt and dating from around 1800 A.C. The sphinx was discovered by the archeologist F.W.M. Petri in 1905, on the high plains of Serabitel Khadem (OUAKNIN, 1997, p. 42), on Mount Sinai, and deciphered in 1916 by A.H. Gardner: he determined that the script was acronymic, each hieroglyph serving as an indication of the first sound of the word. Each hieroglyph corresponded, then, to a word beginning with that sound, which it came to represent. In that way, the sound corresponding to "B" was represented by the hieroglyph of the house at bayit, from which the name of the letter "Bet" is derived. The acronymic script is remarked upon in the first sonnet *Aleph*:

> Each word's initial sound will henceforth be
> inscribed by you, a letter like a seal.

In these twenty-two sonnets, I work with various aspects of the evolution of the alphabet. I fall back, countless times, on the metonymic process, which consists in taking a part for the whole of the hieroglyph, until arriving bit by bit at abstract lines articulating with each other, and sometimes reduced to a single line, as in the example presented by four verses of the sonnet *Hei*, in which the hieroglyph of a man praying is reduced to three parallel lines against a vertical one (the letter E), after the head and the body have been eliminated:

> Then drawing razor deep they cut away
> Both head and body, leaving arms bereft
>
> The vertical turned horizontal now,
> Three strokes in parallel upon a line

In the establishment of abstract lines, one can see a tension between the straight and the curved, with sometimes one predominating, at other times the other, as in the sonnet *Bet*:

> The turning of the arms, the slow advance
> in search of other ways for those straight lines,
> until they come curved back, with breasts as
>   guides,
> the refuge now of other written signs

On the other hand, I note the characteristic of alphabetic systems in which the letters represent consonants and, with the contribution of the Greeks, come to represent vowels as well. The power that the same letter has to represent various sounds is expressed in four lines from the sonnet "Shin", from which the letter "S" is derived:

> Its meager line suggests all hissing sounds,
>
> inscribed on parchment as a shifting sign,
> a symbol for all strident sibilations,
> or simply silent, subtle susurrations.

An example of the representation of vowels by the Greeks can be found, again in sonnet *Bet*:

> Celestial vault, close nestled on your breast,
>
> with intimate companionship's caress,
> immortalizing sheltered utterance,
> vowels join at last their consonant to stay.

A continuous metaphor of the contribution of the Greeks is the contrast between the cosmic monotheistic vision of the Jews, turned toward a G-d who cannot be mentioned:

> It only tells of what their eyes can see.
> It may not touch upon what is divine. (*Zayin*)

And the Hellenic cosmic vision, pagan and earthly, as seen in sonnet *Hei*:

> that seal the borrowed record and allow
>
> the voice to speak on Grecian soil:
> baccants who sow their vowels and consonants in time,
> contrasted in their endless circle dance.

The dissemination of the alphabet achieved by the Phoenicians, starting from Byblos, particularly in their navigations throughout the Mediterranean Sea, is one of the leit-motifs, as in *Gimel*:

> Dissatisfied,
> harassed, you burst forth in a new-made guise,
> and cross the *Mare Nostrum* without fears

Or in *Zayin*:

> A long Phoenician keel with fanning oars
> for seven moons plows through the darkened seas
> and spreads with open palms on alien shores
>
> an indecisive but recorded line.

But most of all, there are the underlying differences between the oral and the written, and the Latin saying *verba volant, scripta manent* (the spoken word flies off, the written remains) pervades the text, as in the sonnet *Kaf*:

a matrix for disseminating change,

as dragonflies ashimmer start to spread
the pollen of new songs, for bards to blend,
so they will not be lost among the dead,
and so the weave of words will never end.

A miracle atemporal in history
unlike all murmured, merely spoken, rhymes
the wind bears off to tombs where silence reigns,

where they lie down in limbo's mystery.

—**Leonor Scliar-Cabral**

Bibliographic Reference

Ouqknin, Marc-Alain. *Les Mystères de l'alphabet*. Paris: Assouline, 1997.

Translating *Consecration of the Aleph Bet*: The Joys of Exigency

Working on the translation of this book into English, both poet and translator shared a love and respect for the challenge imposed by the sonnet form itself. We both embraced the strict demands of that venerable structure first established in thirteenth century Italy. We both felt that the formal qualities are an essential part of the beauty, elegance, and power of the sonnet and should not be abandoned, ignored, or diminished in the interest of a more rigid literal rendition of the text. And so, we struggled together on the English translation of these twenty-two sonnets dedicated to the letters of the Hebrew alphabet. All liberties that the attentive reader may find in the English incarnation of these poems were agreed upon by poet and translator. We were, in fact, co-conspirators, and took mutual delight in finding solutions that would approximate the literal meaning of the original, while satisfying the rigorous demands of the traditional sonnet's iambic pentameter and its various patterns of rhyme. We worked in harmony, having agreed from the beginning that the sonnet's formal qualities of meter and rhyme had to be firmly maintained, that these factors were part and parcel of the beauty of the language, of the music, of our mutual task.

Sometimes finding an equivalent rhyme is easy. In the second stanza of *Yud*, for example, the simple rhyme espaço/abraço is served perfectly by space/embrace, thanks to linguistic Latin roots mingling with Anglo-Saxon after the Norman Invasion. Sometimes, however, one must stretch the dictionary a tiny bit. In *Vav*, for example, the poet rhymed "jogo" with "fogo." The solution was simple: although "fire," the literally correct rendition in English of "fogo," does not rhyme with "game", "flame" does. The part stands for the whole and the translator smiles in relief. English is much less rhyme-rich than the romance languages, so often one takes recourse in some form of slant or partial rhyme. In the first stanza of *Zayin*, for example, the poet rhymes "batalha" (battle) with "navalhas" (blades). One would be hard-pressed to find a rhyme for "battle," but "war," a proper synecdoche, is more amenable. And so we have "sharpened swords", providing an assonantal vowel rhyme for the war they serve.

Of course, end-rhyme is not the only poetic device of concern to the translator. So, when listening to my translation in progress, I seek, when possible, further musical support within the lines. That support can be in the form of a simple repetition, as in "Sweet clasp of honey sweetens…" (*Dalet*). It most often can be found in alliteration (repetition of consonant sounds), or of assonance (repetition of vowel sounds). Here are a few examples drawn from a scattering of these poems: "companionship's caress," (*Bet*), "curve concave," (*Dalet*), "silence…cell…servitude" (*Het*), "stretch…skins… snakes" (*Tet*), "frills…former fripperies" (*Yud*), "bards to bend" and "weave of words" (*Kaf*), "beam…balance…blind" (*Lamed*), "plagues…pestilence…pledge" (*Nun*), "clubs and cudgels" (*Kuf*), and "wash of waves" (*Resh*). Then there are wider spread alliterative effects, as in *Shin*:

> A symbol for all strident sibilations,
> or simply silent, subtle susurrations.

And sometimes one discovers a weave of more than one sound: "slimy sea-bed blankets wrap you round" (*Tzadi*) or "foot by foot, befouled with blood…." (*Tav*), and for that one is especially grateful.

The attentive reader, especially if bilingual, will notice, of course, that not all the inner rhyming techniques are direct echoes from the original. The aim is not to echo each individual poetic device, but to resonate with the cumulative spirit, the feel and the life of the original, so that, in the end, the music of the English recreates the spirit inhabiting the music of the original Portuguese. To both the poet and me, the music of language is the heart of the matter. Let us think of the sonnet, then, as a kind of song, and the melody of that song is being played for you, we hope in harmony, on two distinct instruments: the Portuguese and the English language. We hope you enjoy our duet as much as we enjoyed creating it.

Alexis Levitin
Morrisonville, N.Y., August 2024

About the Author

Leonor Scliar-Cabral is Professor Emerita at the Federal University of Santa Catarina in Brazil. She continues to work as a psycholinguist in the field of literacy training. Her poetry has appeared in Brazil in the following volumes: *Sonnets, Memories of the Sephardim, Of Erotic Senectitude, The Sun Fell on the Guaíba, Consecration of the Aleph Bet*, and *The Book of Joseph*. All of the poems included in her collection *Consecration of the Aleph Bet* have appeared in the following literary magazines: *Amethyst Review, Blue Unicorn, Epoch, Home Planet News, Measure, niv, Oberon Poetry Magazine, Per Contra, Plume*, and *Poetica Magazine*. Poems drawn from her recent *Book of Joseph* have been accepted by *Amethyst, Blue Unicorn, International Poetry Review*, and *Metamorphoses*.

About the Translator

Alexis Levitin has published fifty books of translations, including Clarice Lispector's *Soulstorm* and Eugenio de Andrade's *Forbidden Words*, both from New Directions. His most recent translations of poetry include: from Brazil, five volumes by Salgado Maranhão and two collections by Astrid Cabral; from Portugal, Rosa Alice Branco's *Cattle of the Lord* and Eugenio de Andrade's *Furrows of Thirst*, and from Ecuador, Carmen Vascones' *Outrage*. He is the recipient of two National Endowment for the Arts translation awards and has held Fulbright positions in Portugal, Brazil, and Ecuador. He is Leonor Scliar-Cabral's official translator into English.

The Jewish Poetry Project

jpoetry.us

Ben Yehuda Press

From the Coffee House of Jewish Dreamers: Poems of Wonder and Wandering and the Weekly Torah Portion by Isidore Century

"Isidore Century is a wonderful poet. His poems are funny, deeply observed, without pretension." —*The Jewish Week*

The House at the Center of the World: Poetic Midrash on Sacred Space by Abe Mezrich

"Direct and accessible, Mezrich's midrashic poems often tease profound meaning out of his chosen Torah texts. These poems remind us that our Creator is forgiving, that the spiritual and physical can inform one another, and that the supernatural can be carried into the everyday."
—Yehoshua November, author of *God's Optimism*

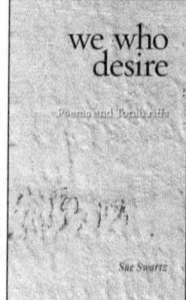

we who desire: Poems and Torah riffs by Sue Swartz

"Sue Swartz does magnificent acrobatics with the Torah. She takes the English that's become staid and boring, and adds something that's new and strange and exciting. These are poems that leave a taste in your mouth, and you walk away from them thinking, what did I just read? Oh, yeah. It's the Bible."
—Matthue Roth, author, *Yom Kippur A Go-Go*

Open My Lips: Prayers and Poems by Rachel Barenblat

"Barenblat's God is a personal God—one who lets her cry on His shoulder, and who rocks her like a colicky baby. These poems bridge the gap between the ineffable and the human. This collection will bring comfort to those with a religion of their own, as well as those seeking a relationship with some kind of higher power."
—Satya Robyn, author, *The Most Beautiful Thing*

Words for Blessing the World: Poems in Hebrew and English by Herbert J. Levine

"These writings express a profoundly earth-based theology in a language that is clear and comprehensible. These are works to study and learn from."
—Rodger Kamenetz, author, *The Jew in the Lotus*

Shiva Moon: Poems by Maxine Silverman

"The poems, deeply felt, are spare, spoken in a quiet but compelling voice, as if we were listening in to her inner life. This book is a precious record of the transformation saying Kaddish can bring."
—Howard Schwartz, author, *The Library of Dreams*

is: heretical Jewish blessings and poems by Yaakov Moshe (Jay Michaelson)

"Finally, Torah that speaks to and through the lives we are actually living: expanding the tent of holiness to embrace what has been cast out, elevating what has been kept down, advancing what has been held back, reveling in questions, revealing contradictions."
—Eden Pearlstein, aka eprhyme

Texts to the Holy: Poems
by Rachel Barenblat

"These poems are remarkable, radiating a love of God that is full bodied, innocent, raw, pulsating, hot, drunk. I can hardly fathom their faith but am grateful for the vistas they open. I will sit with them, and invite you to do the same."
—Merle Feld, author of *A Spiritual Life*

The Sabbath Bee: Love Songs to Shabbat
by Wilhelmina Gottschalk

"Torah, say our sages, has seventy faces. As these prose poems reveal, so too does Shabbat. Here we meet Shabbat as familiar housemate, as the child whose presence transforms a family, as a spreading tree, as an annoying friend who insists on being celebrated, as a woman, as a man, as a bee, as the ocean."
—Rachel Barenblat, author, *The Velveteen Rabbi's Haggadah*

All the Holes Line Up: Poems and Translations by Zackary Sholem Berger

"Spare and precise, Berger's poems gaze unflinchingly at—but also celebrate—human imperfection in its many forms. And what a delight that Berger also includes in this collection a handful of his resonant translations of some of the great Yiddish poets." —Yehoshua November, author of *God's Optimism* and *Two World Exist*

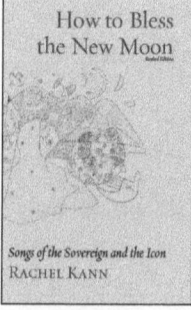

How to Bless the New Moon: Songs of the Sovereign and the Icon
by Rachel Kann

"Rachel Kann is a master wordsmith. Her poems are rich in content, packed with life's wisdom and imbued with soul. May this collection of her work enable more of the world to enjoy her offerings."
—Sarah Yehudit Schneider, author of *You Are What You Hate*

Into My Garden
by David Caplan

"The beauty of Caplan's book is that it is not polemical. It does not set out to win an argument or ask you whether you've put your tefillin on today. These gentle poems invite the reader into one person's profound, ambiguous religious experience."
—*The Jewish Review of Books*

Between the Mountain and the Land is the Lesson: Poetic Midrash on Sacred Community by Abe Mezrich

"Abe Mezrich cuts straight back to the roots of the Midrashic tradition, sermonizing as a poet, rather than idealogue. Best of all, Abe knows how to ask questions and avoid the obvious answers."
—Jake Marmer, author, *Jazz Talmud*

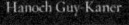

NOKADDISH: Poems in the Void
by Hanoch Guy Kaner

"A subversive, midrashic play with meanings—specifically Jewish meanings, and then the reversal and negation of these meanings."
—Robert G. Margolis

An Added Soul: Poems for a New Old Religion
by Herbert J. Levine

"Herbert J. Levine's lovely poems swing wide the double doors of English and Hebrew and open on the awe of being. Clear and direct, at ease in both tongues, these lyrics embrace a holiness unyoked from myth and theistic searching."
—Lynn Levin, author, *The Minor Virtues*

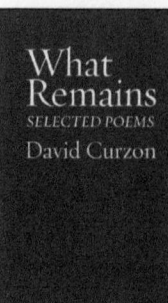

What Remains
by David Curzon

"Aphoristic, ekphrastic, and precise revelations animate WHAT REMAINS. In his stunning rewriting of Psalm 1 and other biblical passages, Curzon shows himself to be a fabricator, a collector, and an heir to the literature, arts, and wisdom traditions of the planet."
—Alicia Ostriker, author of *The Volcano and After*

The Shortest Skirt in Shul
by Sass Oron

"These poems exuberantly explore gender, Torah, the masks we wear, and the way our bodies (and the ways we wear them) at once threaten stable narratives, and offer the kind of liberation that saves our lives."
—Alicia Jo Rabins, author of *Divinity School*, composer of *Girls In Trouble*

Walking Triptychs
by Ilya Gutner

These are poems from when I walked about Shanghai and thought about the meaning of the Holocaust.

Book of Failed Salvation
by Julia Knobloch

"These beautiful poems express a tender longing for spiritual, physical, and emotional connection. They detail a life in movement—across distances, faith, love, and doubt."
—David Caplan, author, *Into My Garden*

Daily Blessings: Poems on Tractate Berakhot
by Hillel Broder

"Hillel Broder does not just write poetry about the Talmud; he also draws out the Talmud's poetry, finding lyricism amidst legality and re-setting the Talmud's rich images like precious gems in end-stopped lines of verse."
—Ilana Kurshan, author of *If All the Seas Were Ink*

The Missing Jew: Poems 1976-2022
by Rodger Kamenetz

"How does Rodger Kamenetz manage to have so singular a voice and at the same time precisely encapsulate the world view of an entire generation (also mine) of text-hungry American Jews born in the middle of the twentieth century?"
—Jacqueline Osherow, author, *Ultimatum from Paradise* and *My Lookalike at the Krishna Temple: Poems*

The Red Door: A dark fairy tale told in poems
by Shawn Harris

"THE RED DOOR, like its poet author Shawn C. Harris, transcends genres and identities. It is an exploration in crossing worlds. It brings together poetry and story telling, imagery and life events, spirit and body, the real and the fantastic, Jewish past and Jewish present, to spin one tale."
—Einat Wilf, author, *The War of Return*

The Matter of Families
by Robert Deluty

"Robert Deluty's career-spanning collection of New and Selected poems captures the essence of his work: the power of love, joy, and connection, all tied together with the poet's glorious sense of humor. This book is Deluty's masterpiece."
—Richard M. Berlin, M.D., author of *Freud on My Couch*

There Is No Place Without You
by Maya Bernstein

"Bernstein's poems brim with energy and sound, moving the reader around a world mapped by motherhood, contemplation, religion, and the effects of illness on the body and spirit. Her language is lyrical, delicate, and poised; her lens is lucid and original."
—Anthony Anaxagorou, author of *After the Formalities*

Torah Limericks
by Rhonda Rosenheck

"Rhonda Rosenheck knows the Hebrew Bible, and she knows that it can stand up to the sometimes silly, sometimes snarky, but always insightful scholarship packed into each one of these interpretive jewels."
—Rabbi Hillel Norry

Words for a Dazzling Firmament
by Abe Mezrich

"Mezrich is a cultivated craftsman: interpretively astute, sonically deliberate, and spiritually cunning."

—Zohar Atkins, author of *Nineveh*

Everything Thaws
by R. B. Lemberg

"Full of glacier-sharp truths, and moments revealed between words like bodies beneath melting permafrost. As it becomes increasingly plain how deeply our world is shaped by war and climate change and grief and anger, articulating that shape feels urgent and necessary."
—Ruthanna Emrys, author of *A Half-Built Garden*

Bits and Pieces
by Edward Pomerantz

"A stunning tapestry of family life in the 40s and 50s. Like all great poetry, Pomerantz's work expands after reading. Each poem is exquisitely structured, often with a stunning ending, into a masterful whole."
—Alan Ziegler, editor of SHORT: *An International Anthology*

Old Shul
by Pinny Bulman

"Nostalgia gives way to a tender theology, a softly chuckling illumination from within the heart of/as a beautiful, broken sanctuary, somehow both gritty and fragile, grimy and iridescent – not unlike faith itself."
—Jake Marmer, author of *Cosmic Diaspora*

Poems for a Cartoon Mouse
by Andrew Burt

"Andrew Burt's poetry magnifies the vanishingly small line between danger and safety. This collection asks whether order is an illusion that veils chaos, or vice-versa, juxtaposing images from the Bible with animated films."
—Ari Shapiro, host of NPR's *All Things Considered*

Feet In L.A., But My Womb Lives In Jerusalem, My Breath In Vermont
by Lori Levy

"Reading through Lori Levy's new book of poems takes my breath away. With no pretense whatsoever, they leap, alive, from the page until this reader felt as if she were living Levy's life. How does the author do it?"
—Mary Jo Balistreri, author of *Still*

Ode to the Dove: *An illustrated, bilingual edition of a Yiddish poem by Abraham Sutzkever*
Zackary Sholem Berger, translator
Liora Ostroff, Illustrator

"An elegant volume for lovers of poetry."
—Justin Cammy, translator of *Sutzkever, From the Vilna Ghetto to Nuremberg: Memoir and Testimony*

poem hashavua: A Personal Engagement with the Weekly Torah Portion in Poems and Pictures
by Lexie Botzum et al.

"Giving voice to unarticulated interpretations and stories, weaving yourself into the text, is a way of claiming ownership."
—from the author's Introduction

Duets on Psalms:
Drawing New Meaning From Ancient Words
by Jack Riemer & Elie Spitz

"Two remarkable rabbis breathe new life into the ancient words of The Book of Psalms. A literary journey filled with faith, wisdom, hope, healing, meaning and inspiration."
—Rabbi Naomi Levy, author of *Einstein and the Rabbi* and *To Begin Again*

Chrysalis Summer: Poems of Transformation
by Suzanne Brody

"Each page offers a unique surprise. Each poem, with its own unique flavor, elicits a distinct feeling ranging from sweet, amused wonderings to spicy cries of frustration, pain, and longing, to simply savory, enjoyable nuggets. The thoughts and emotions of one woman who plays many roles—teacher, mother, rabbi, and artist."
—Dori Weinstein, author of the YaYa & YoYo series"

So Many Warm Words
Selections from the Poetry of Rosa Nevadovska

A bilingual edition of Yiddish poems translated by Merle L. Bachman

www.ingramcontent.com/pod-product-compliance
Lightning Source LLC
LaVergne TN
LVHW041339080426
835512LV00006B/540